Washington Monument

Aaron Carr

www.av2books.com

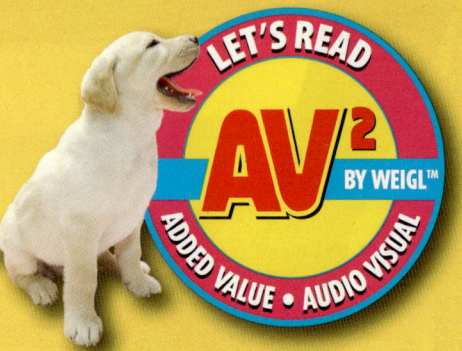

Go to www.av2books.com, and enter this book's unique code.

BOOK CODE

X220472

AV² by Weigl brings you media enhanced books that support active learning.

AV² provides enriched content that supplements and complements this book. Weigl's AV² books strive to create inspired learning and engage young minds in a total learning experience.

Your AV² Media Enhanced books come alive with...

Audio
Listen to sections of the book read aloud.

Video
Watch informative video clips.

Embedded Weblinks
Gain additional information for research.

Try This!
Complete activities and hands-on experiments.

Key Words
Study vocabulary, and complete a matching word activity.

Quizzes
Test your knowledge.

Slide Show
View images and captions, and prepare a presentation.

... and much, much more!

Published by AV² by Weigl
350 5th Avenue, 59th Floor New York, NY 10118
Website: www.av2books.com   www.weigl.com

Copyright ©2014 AV² by Weigl
All rights reserved. No part of this publication may be reproduced, stored in a retrieval system, or transmitted in any form or by any means, electronic, mechanical, photocopying, recording, or otherwise, without the prior written permission of the publisher.

                    Library of Congress Cataloging-in-Publication Data
Carr, Aaron.
Washington Monument / Aaron Carr.
    p. cm. -- (American icons)
ISBN 978-1-62127-205-2 (hardcover : alk. paper) -- ISBN 978-1-62127-209-0 (softcover : alk. paper)
1. Washington Monument (Washington, D.C.)--Juvenile literature. 2. Washington, George, 1732-1799--Monuments--Washington (D.C.)--Juvenile literature. 3. Washington (D.C.)--Buildings, structures, etc.--Juvenile literature. I. Title.
F203.4.W3C29 2014
975.3--dc23
                             2012044827

Printed in the United States of America in North Mankato, Minnesota
1 2 3 4 5 6 7 8 9 0   16 15 14 13 12

122012
WEP301112

Senior Editor: Aaron Carr
Designer: Mandy Christiansen

Every reasonable effort has been made to trace ownership and to obtain permission to reprint copyright material. The publishers would be pleased to have any errors or omissions brought to their attention so that they may be corrected in subsequent printings.

Weigl acknowledges Getty Images as the primary image supplier for this title.

CONTENTS

2 AV² Book Code
4 What is the Washington Monument?
7 A National Symbol
8 Planning the Monument
11 On Hold
12 Building the Monument
15 Ring Around the Tower
16 The Tallest Tower
19 View from the Top
20 Washington Monument Today
22 Washington Monument Facts
24 Key Words/Log on to www.av2books.com

What is the Washington Monument?

The Washington Monument is a tall stone tower. It is a part of the National Mall in Washington, D.C.

A National Symbol

The Washington Monument was made to honor George Washington. He was the first president of the United States.

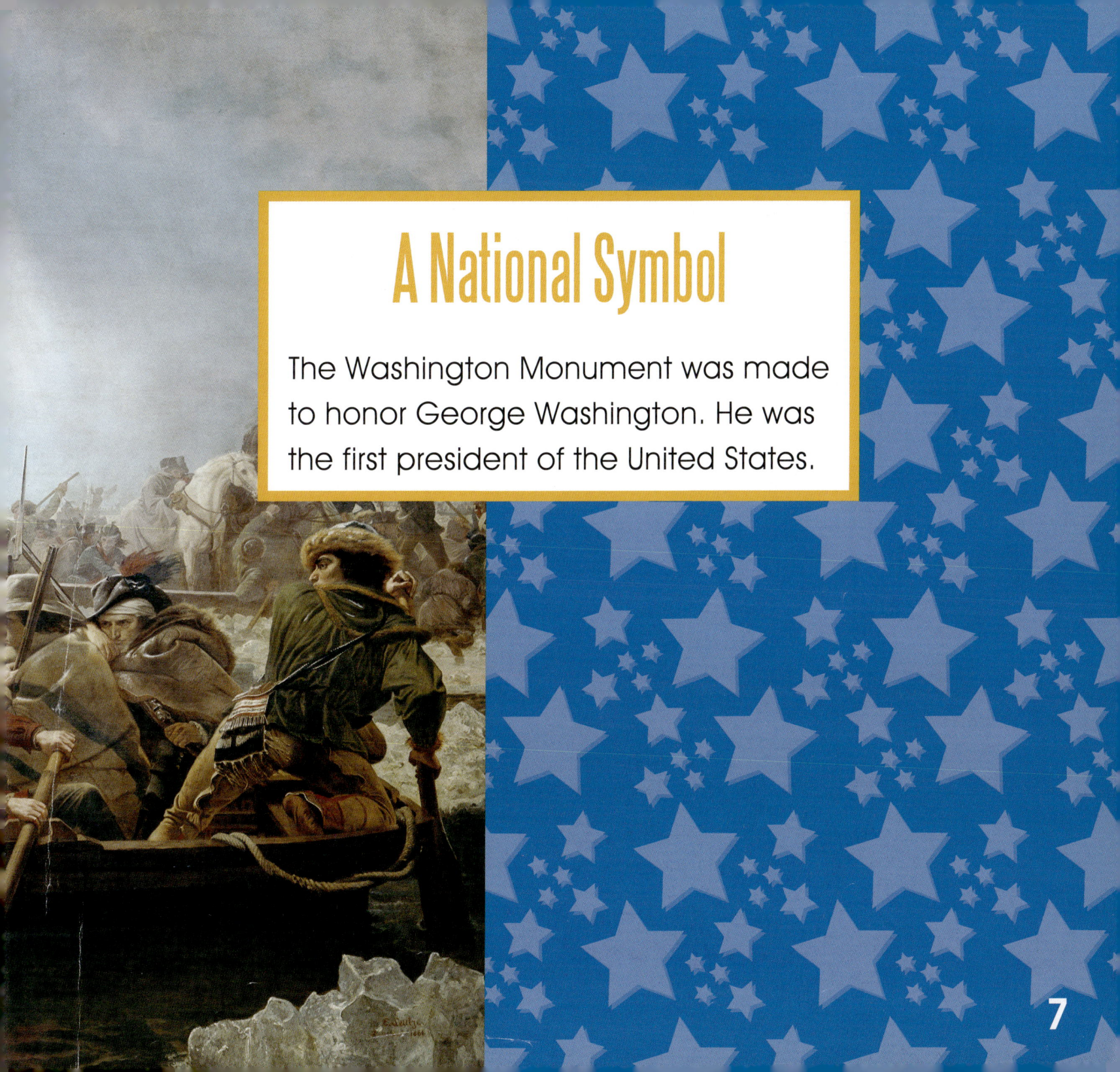

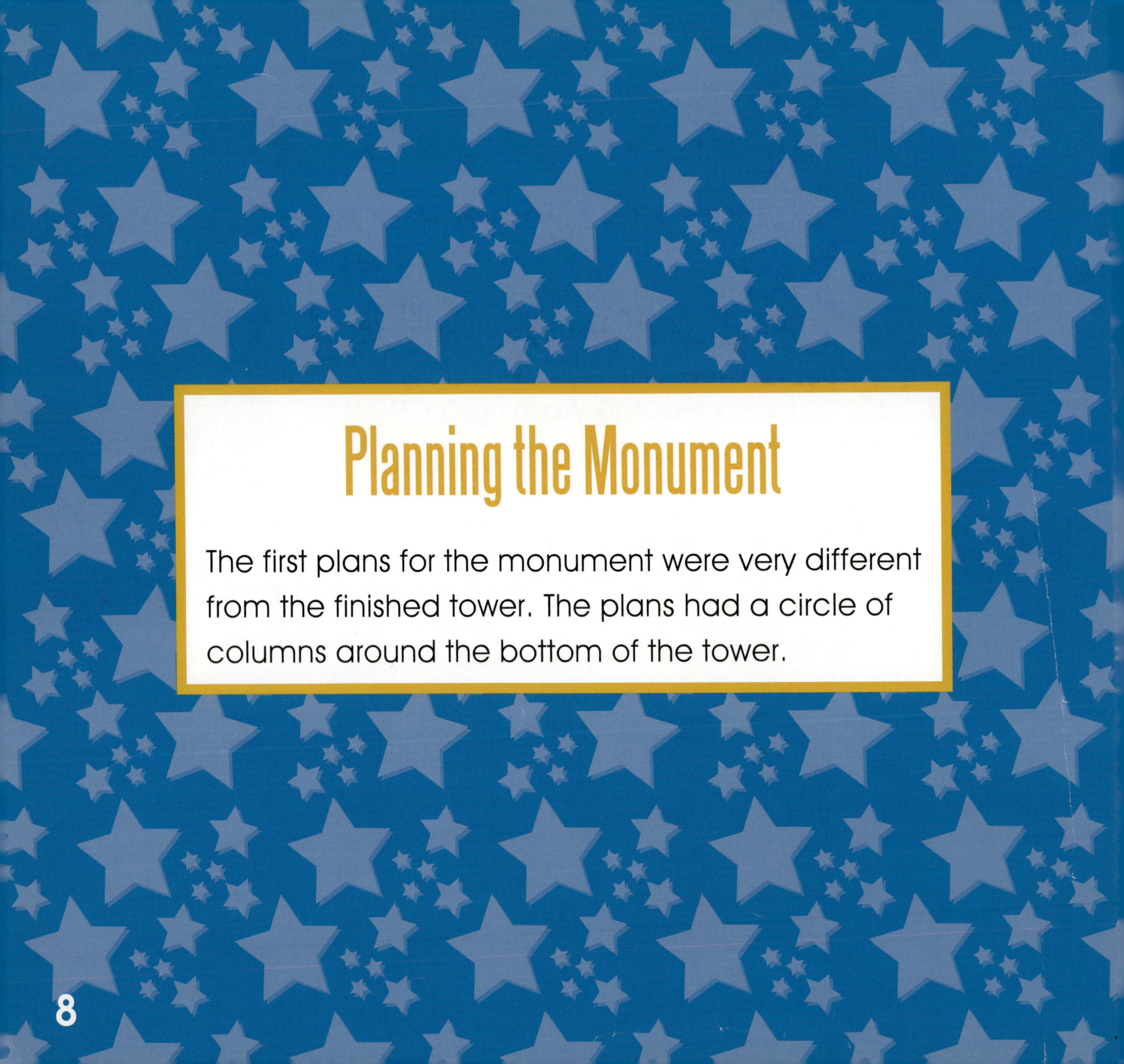

Planning the Monument

The first plans for the monument were very different from the finished tower. The plans had a circle of columns around the bottom of the tower.

On Hold

Work on the monument began in 1884 but stopped 10 years later. The monument was only half finished. Work did not start again for more than 20 years.

Building the Monument

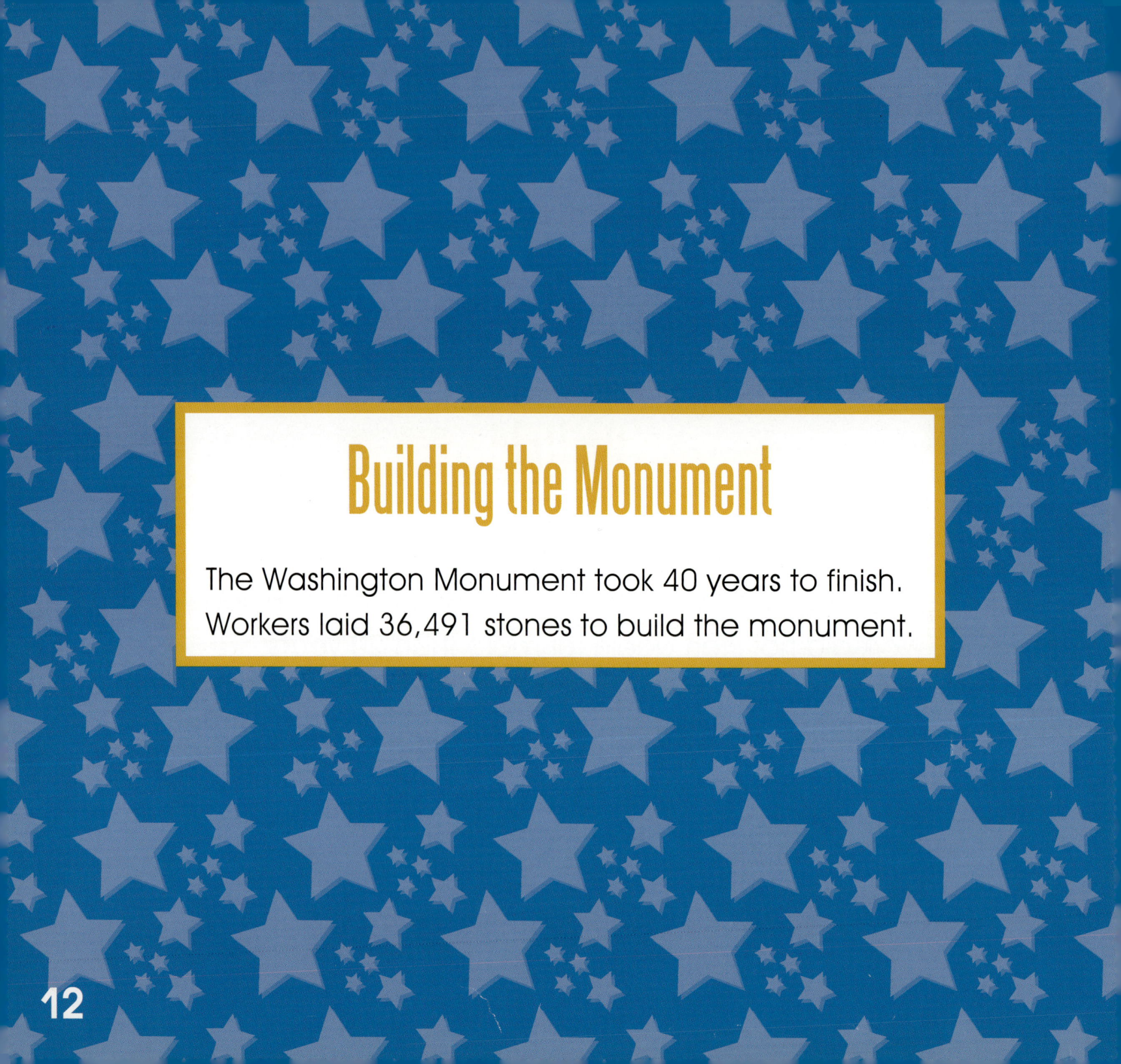

The Washington Monument took 40 years to finish. Workers laid 36,491 stones to build the monument.

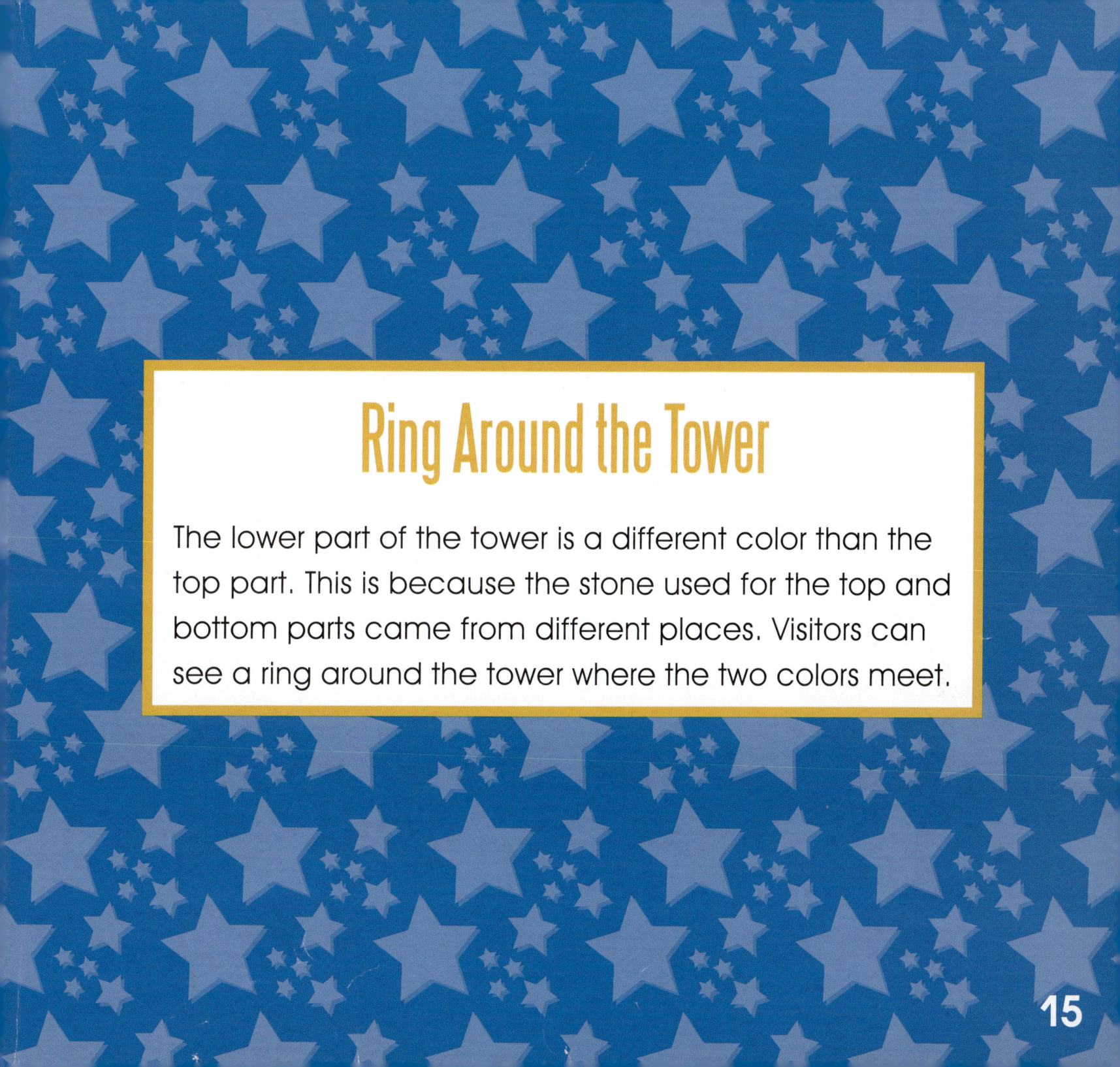

Ring Around the Tower

The lower part of the tower is a different color than the top part. This is because the stone used for the top and bottom parts came from different places. Visitors can see a ring around the tower where the two colors meet.

The Tallest Tower

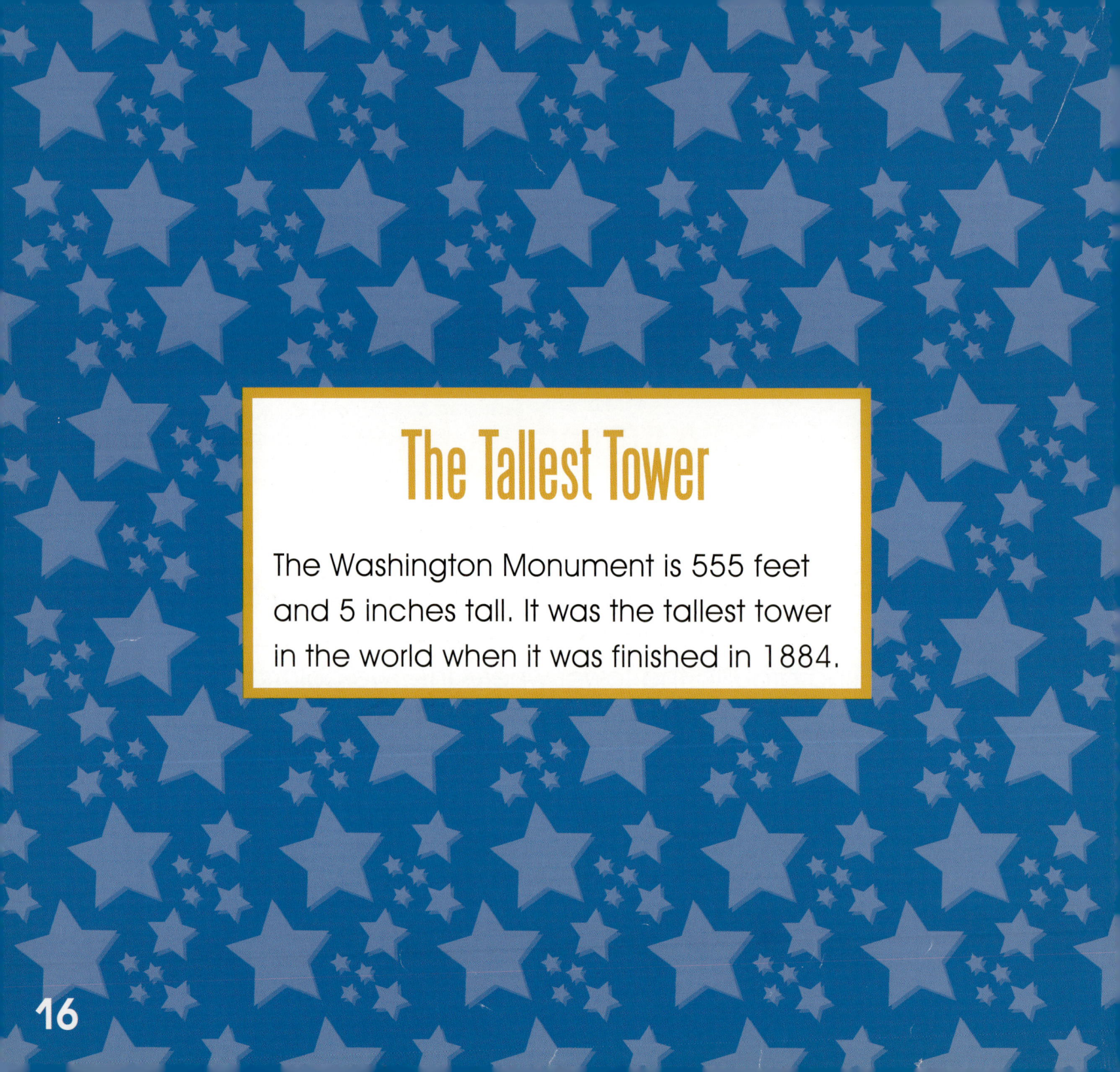

The Washington Monument is 555 feet and 5 inches tall. It was the tallest tower in the world when it was finished in 1884.

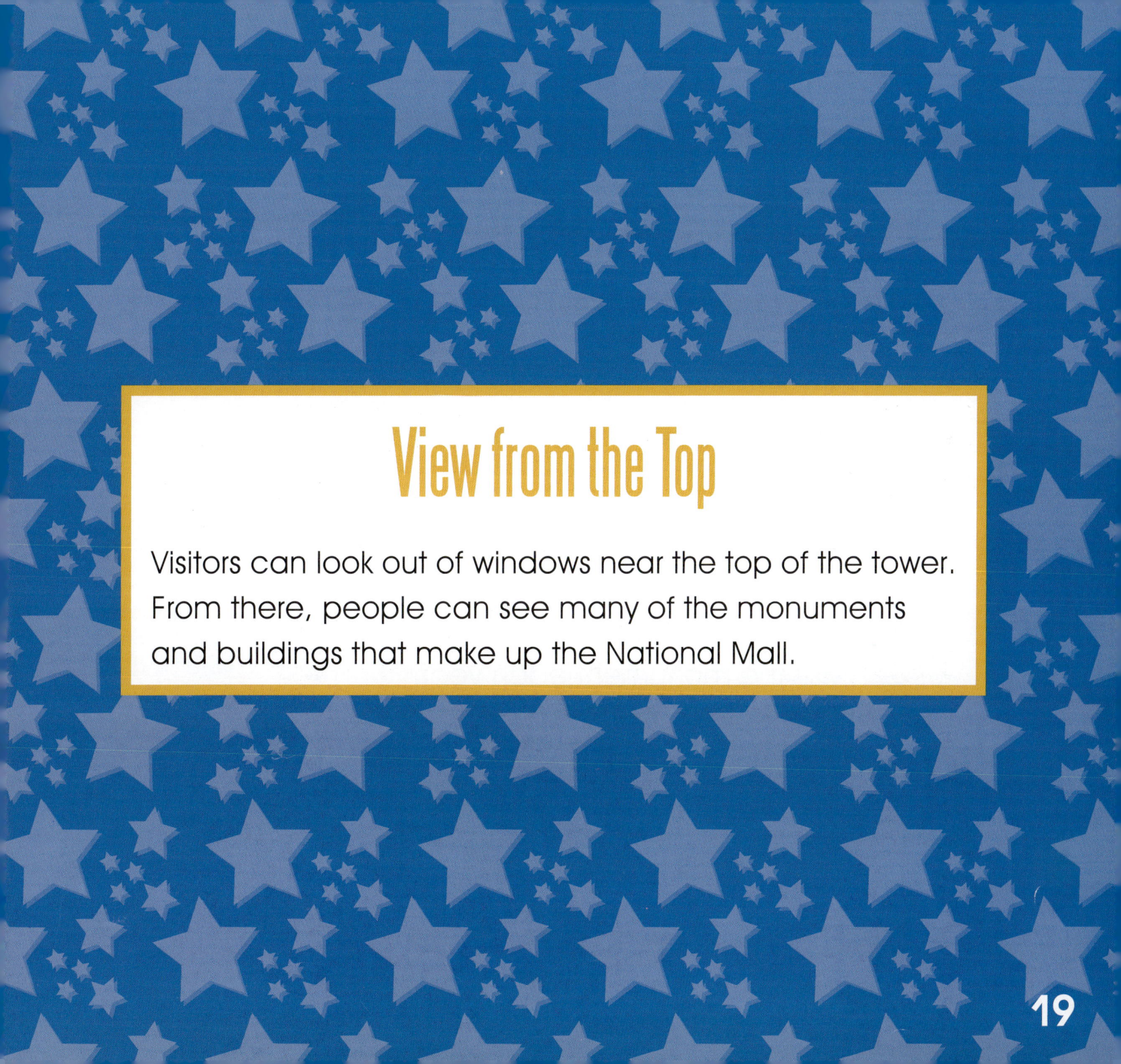

View from the Top

Visitors can look out of windows near the top of the tower. From there, people can see many of the monuments and buildings that make up the National Mall.

Washington Monument Today

The Washington Monument is one of the best-known buildings in the United States. Millions of people from around the world visit the monument each year.

WASHINGTON MONUMENT FACTS

These pages provide detailed information that expands on the interesting facts found in the book. These pages are intended to be used by adults to help young readers round out their knowledge of each national symbol featured in the *American Icons* series.

Pages 4–5

What is the Washington Monument? The Washington Monument is an Egyptian-style obelisk with a pyramid on top. It is 55 feet (16.8 meters) square at the base and narrows toward the top. The walls are also thicker at the base. They are 15 feet (4.6 m) thick at the base and 18 inches (46 centimeters) at the top.

Pages 6–7

A National Symbol George Washington is one of the most prominent figures in American history. He led the Continental Army against the British during the American Revolution. He was later chosen to be the first president of the United States. Washington is called The Father of Our Country. He presided over the convention that led to the signing of the Constitution.

Pages 8–9

Planning the Monument In 1836, architect Robert Mills won a contest to design the Washington Monument. His design called for a 600-foot (183-m) tall obelisk standing on a circular base 250 feet (76 m) in diameter and 100 feet (30.5 m) high. The base would feature a colonnade around the outside with 30 spaces set aside for statues of prominent Americans.

Pages 10–11

On Hold Construction on the monument began when the cornerstone was laid on July 4, 1848. However, funding ran out in 1854, and work on the monument came to a halt. It was only 152 feet (46 m) tall. In 1876, Congress approved new funding. The Army Corps of Engineers took over the project, but they altered the design to save money. Construction began again in 1880.

JUL 2014

Pages 12–13 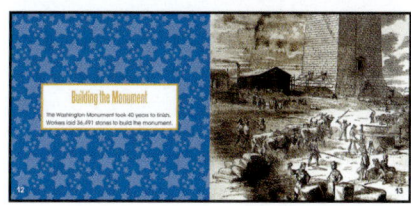 **Building the Monument** The 3,300-pound (1,500-kilogram) capstone was placed on top of the obelisk on December 6, 1884. With the outside complete, the interior was finished and a steam elevator was added to take people to the top of the obelisk. The monument was opened to the public in 1888.

Pages 14–15 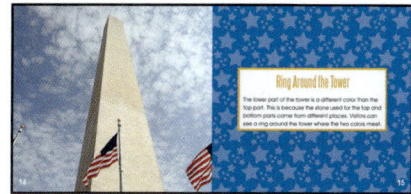 **Ring Around the Tower** When workers finished the construction of the Washington Monument, they could not match the color of marble stones that covered the outside walls. This is because the new stones came from a different quarry than the original stones. Now, there is a change in color between the older part at the bottom of the tower and newer part at the top.

Pages 16–17 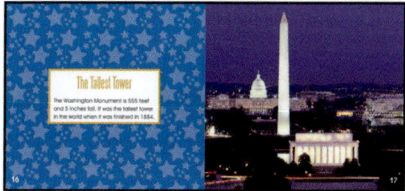 **The Tallest Tower** At 555 feet, 5 inches (169 m), the Washington Monument is the tallest building in Washington, D.C. When the external structure of the monument was finished in 1884, it was the tallest humanmade structure in the world. It remains the world's tallest masonry structure today.

Pages 18–19 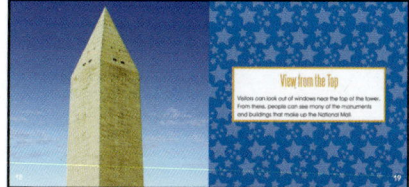 **View from the Top** An observation area is located 500 feet (152 m) up the tower. From there, visitors can see much of the city, including the Lincoln Memorial, the Jefferson Memorial, the White House, and the Capitol. Visitors can take an elevator to the viewing area. There are also 897 stairs leading to the top, but they are closed to the public.

Pages 20–21  **Washington Monument Today** The Washington Monument is one of the most iconic structures in the United States. More than 25 million people visit the National Mall each year. In August 2011, an earthquake shook the east coast. The earthquake caused millions of dollars in damage to the Washington Monument. The monument was closed for repairs until 2014.

KEY WORDS

Research has shown that as much as 65 percent of all written material published in English is made up of 300 words. These 300 words cannot be taught using pictures or learned by sounding them out. They must be recognized by sight. This book contains 57 common sight words to help young readers improve their reading fluency and comprehension. This book also teaches young readers several important content words, such as nouns. These words are paired with pictures to aid in learning and improve understanding.

Page	Sight Words First Appearance
4	a, in, is, it, of, part, the, what
7	first, he, made, to, was
8	around, different, for, from, had, very, were
11	again, began, but, did, later, more, not, on, only, than, work, years
12	took
15	and, because, came, can, places, see, this, two, used, where
16	feet, when, world
19	look, make, many, near, out, people, that, there, up
20	each, one

Page	Content Words First Appearance
4	National Mall; stone; tower; Washington, D.C.; Washington Monument
7	George Washington, president, symbol United States
8	bottom, circle, columns, monument, plans
12	workers
15	color, ring, top, visitors
16	inches
19	buildings, view, windows

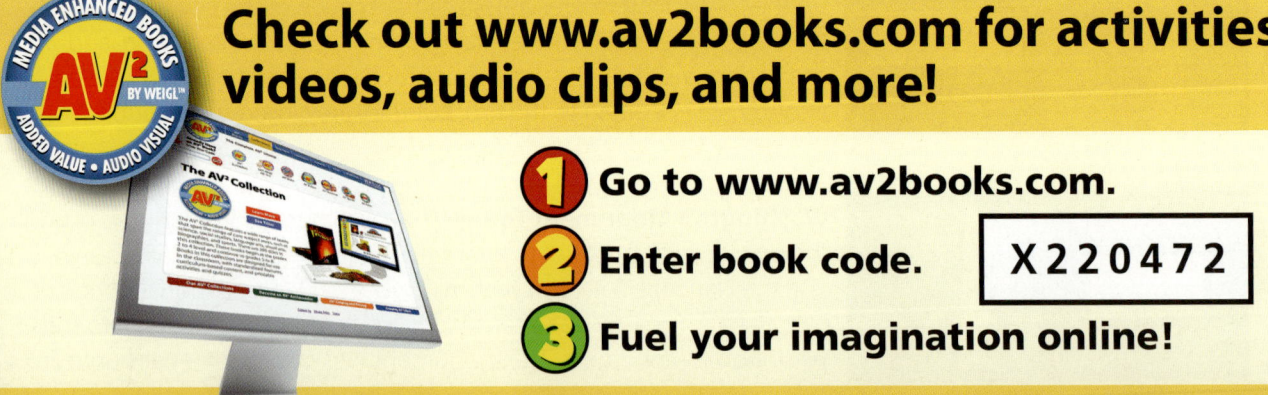

Check out www.av2books.com for activities, videos, audio clips, and more!

1. Go to www.av2books.com.
2. Enter book code. X 2 2 0 4 7 2
3. Fuel your imagination online!

www.av2books.com